Members Favourite
Mediterranean
Recipes

Mediterranean
Contents

Bon Appétit!

- Italian Eggs with Ciabatta — 8
- Hearty Minestrone — 9
- Potato Scone Pizza with Roasted Veg — 10
- French Bread Pepperoni Pizza — 11
- Ham & Garlic Mushroom Pizza — 12

Mama Mia Pasta

- Pasta with Chorizo & Peppers — 14
- Chicken, Ham & Artichoke Pasta Bake — 15
- Linguine Zarina — 16
- Tagliatelle Verdi — 17
- Pasta Puttanesca — 18
- Spaghetti Milanese — 19
- Baked Penne — 20

Fish Fiesta

- Moules Marinières — 22
- Sole & Spinach Roulades — 23
- Italian Fish Topper — 24
- Seafood Paella — 25
- Trout with Almonds — 26
- Morroccan Fish Stew — 27

Poultry with Passion

- Piri Piri Chicken — 29
- Spinach & Feta Stuffed Chicken — 30
- Chicken Cordon Bleu — 31
- Greek Lemon Chicken — 32
- Tuscan Turkey Paesana — 33
- Cheat's Chicken Provencale — 34
- Turkey Koftas — 35

Excellent **Entrées**

- Lamb with Apricots & Couscous — 37
- Beef Bourguignon — 38
- Saltimbocca — 39
- Pork Escalopes Marsala — 40
- Beef Olives — 41
- Moussaka — 42

Oooh La La! **Desserts**

- Crêpes Suzette-style — 44
- Cappuccino Cream — 45
- Pear & Ratafia Flan — 46
- Black Cherry Zabaglione — 47
- Stuffed Peaches — 48

We always listen to what our members are saying, and one thing they frequently mention is how much they love Mediterranean-style food. Many tell us that being able to enjoy it guilt free is what helps them stick with their weight loss Eating Plan.

Well this collection of "Mediterranean" favourites will fit the bill nicely. Some are your favourites from past Eating Plans which you have asked us to revive, and some are new recipes which we have no doubt will become firm favourites of the future.

All recipes have been counted to fit into the Positive Eating Plan. You'll find calories, Checks and fat gram values for all recipes - minus "free" foods, of course! Most recipes also include "serving suggestions", and we give separate counts when these are added to the recipe. We also tell you what type of meal it is, for those of you who prefer to "Choose Meals" rather than "Choose Checks".

Do check out the "Free Foods" list and "Mediterranean" Check List so you can include even more variety and add those essential personal touches.

Enjoy - we're sure you will!

• Calories Checks Fat Grams

Free Foods

Herbs and spices may be used freely on the Positive Eating Plan, as long as they don't have added oil.

Small quantities of seasonings such as soy sauce, beef or yeast extract, stock cubes and a light spray of oil are also "free".

Whenever "free" salad or vegetables are mentioned, you may choose from the following:

Alfalfa sprouts	French beans (greenbeans)
Artichoke hearts	Jerusalem artichokes
Asparagus	Kale
Aubergine	Leeks
Baby sweetcorn	Lettuce, all types
Bamboo shoots	Mangetout/snow peas
Beansprouts	Marrow
Beetroot	Mooli
Bok choi/pak choi	Mushrooms
Broccoli	Okra
Brussels sprouts	Onions, all types
Cabbage, all types	Peppers, all colours
Calabrese	Pumpkin
Carrots	Radishes
Cauliflower	Runner beans
Celeriac	Salsify
Celery	Sauerkraut
Chard	Spinach
Chicory	Spring greens
Chinese leaves	Squash, all types
Christophene (cho-cho)	Sugar snap peas
Courgettes	Swede
Cress	Tomatoes
Cucumber	Turnips
Endive	Water chestnuts
Fennel	Watercress

Remember - "free" foods do not need to be counted on the Positive Eating Plan!

Mediterranean
Check List

1 breadstick	20	**1**	0
50g ciabatta bread	130	**5**	2
50g foccacia bread	155	**6**	7
50g french bread	130	**5**	1
60g pitta bread	150	**6**	1
30g dry weight/75g boiled weight pasta	100	**4**	0.5
40g raw weight/75g boiled weight fresh egg pasta	100	**4**	1.5
3 lasagne sheets	210	**8**	1
30g dry weight/75g boiled weight rice	100	**4**	0.5
1 Napolina Long-life mini pizza base	220	**9**	2
30g mozzarella	90	**4**	6
30g mozzarella light	60	**2.5**	3
30g feta	90	**4**	7
30g halloumi	90	**4**	7
25g mascarpone	115	**5**	12
25g ricotta	50	**2**	4
10ml dspn grated parmesan	20	**1**	2
1 tsp olive oil	40	**1.5**	4
1 medium egg	80	**3**	6
Canned tomatoes		free food	
1 medium peach	50	**2**	0
1 fresh fig	25	**1**	0
300g/10 oz wedge of melon, with skin	50	**2**	0
85g/3 oz grapes	50	**2**	0
5 large olives	25	**1**	2
Capers		free food	
Balsamic vinegar		free food	
1 heaped tsp pesto	60	**2.5**	6
2 tbsp wine	20	**1**	0
1 tbsp marsala or sherry	20	**1**	0
1 Doria amaretti biscuit	25	**1**	0.5
2 baby ratafia biscuits	25	**1**	0

nb: values are typical averages across brands and types

Italian Eggs with Ciabatta

Serves 1

per serving

300   **12** 13

or 1 Quick Meal

1 courgette, sliced
85g/3 oz cherry tomatoes, halved
1 tbsp fresh basil leaves, torn
1 tsp olive oil
Salt and pepper
1 medium Lion Quality egg
15g/½ oz half-fat cheddar, grated
60g/2 oz warm ciabatta bread

Pre-heat oven to 200°C/gas mark 6.

In an ovenproof dish, toss together the courgettes, tomatoes, basil, oil and salt and pepper.

Bake 20 minutes, or until courgettes are pale golden.

Make a well in the centre of the vegetables and carefully break the egg into the hole. Sprinkle over the grated cheese and bake a further 10 minutes, or until egg is done to your liking.

Serve with the warm ciabatta bread, or toast lightly if preferred.

Mediterranean
Hearty Minestrone

per serving   250 **10** 4

or 1 Booster Quick Meal

1 medium onion, chopped
1 carrot, chopped
1 stick celery, finely sliced
1 clove garlic, peeled and chopped
900ml/1½ pints chicken or vegetable stock
2 tbsp tomato purée
½ tsp mixed herbs or Italian seasoning
60g/2 oz savoy cabbage, finely sliced
60g/2 oz frozen sliced green beans
60g/2 oz small soup pasta shapes
Salt and black pepper
2 dspn grated parmesan cheese
2 x 60g/2 oz crusty rolls or 115g/4 oz crusty bread

Place the onion, carrot, celery, garlic, stock, tomato purée and herbs into a large saucepan. Stir together and bring to the boil. Turn down heat, cover and simmer 15 minutes.

Add cabbage, green beans and pasta shapes, return to the boil then simmer 8-10 minutes or until pasta is cooked. Stir frequently to prevent pasta from sticking to base of pan. Season to taste.

Serve each person with half the soup topped with 1 dspn grated parmesan cheese, accompanied by 1 crusty roll or half the crusty bread.

Mediterranean
Potato Scone Pizza with Roasted Vegetables & Mozzarella

Serves 1

per serving   310   **12** (4)

or 1 Quick Meal

1 small onion, sliced thinly in rings
Handful of frozen or fresh sliced peppers
Spray oil
1 tomato, sliced
1 mushroom, thinly sliced
150g/5 oz potato, boiled, cooled
4 rounded dspn flour
Salt and black pepper
1 dspn skimmed milk
30g/1 oz half-fat mozzarella
Small pinch of oregano or mixed herbs

Pre-heat oven to 200°C/gas mark 6.

Spray onions and peppers with oil and roast approx. 20-25 minutes. Add tomato and mushroom for last 5 minutes. Meanwhile, mash the potato. Mix in the flour, salt and pepper. Add the skimmed milk to form a dough. Roll or pat out on a lightly floured board to a circle approx. 15cm/6 inches dia.

Spray a frying pan with oil, heat then place dough in pan. Cook gently until browned underneath. Place pan under heated grill to cook top. Finely shred mozzarella. Place roasted vegetables over scone base and season. Scatter over mozzarella and herbs. Return to grill until cheese melts.

Serving suggestion

For a simpler version, make potato scone base as above. Scatter with thinly sliced "free" vegetables of choice and 45g/1½ oz half-fat grated cheddar. Brown under grill and serve with "free" salad.

per serving   375   **15** (7)

or 1 Main Meal

Mediterranean

French Bread Pepperoni Pizza

Serves 4

per serving   305   **12**   13

or 1 Quick Meal

200g/7 oz baton or half-baguette French bread
4 dspn tomato purée
Oregano, marjoram or mixed herbs
115g/4 oz half-fat cheddar, grated
100g pack sliced pepperoni
"Free" salad to serve

Pre-heat oven to 200°C/gas mark 6.

Cut the bread in half down, then across, to form 4 "bases".

With crust side down, spread each base on the bread side with 1 dspn tomato purée. Sprinkle with a small pinch of herbs and top each with quarter of the grated cheese and quarter of the pepperoni slices.

Bake approximately 10-15 minutes, or until bases are crisp and cheese melted.

Serve with "free" salad.

Individual Ham & Garlic Mushroom Pizza

Serves 1

per serving   310   **12** 7

or 1 Quick Meal

2-3 mushrooms
1 dspn tomato purée
1 Napolina long-life Mini Pizza Base
30g/1 oz wafer-thin or lean canned ham
30g/1 oz Boursin Light Garlic & Herb Soft Cheese
"Free" salad to serve

Pre-heat oven to 210°C/gas mark 7.

Cut mushrooms across horizontally, to make circles and poach in water 2-3 minutes.

Spread tomato purée over pizza base. Chop ham and scatter over base. Drain mushrooms and arrange over ham.

Bake 8 minutes. Remove from oven and spread small dabs of Boursin over the mushrooms. Warm under grill about 30 seconds to 1 minute, but do not allow to dry out.

Serve with "free" salad.

Mediterranean
Pasta with Chorizo & Peppers

Serves 2

per serving   375   **15** (12)

or 1 Main Meal

1 small onion, sliceed
150g/5 oz frozen sliced mixed peppers
Spray oil
400g can tomatoes, chopped
1 tbsp tomato purée
1 tsp paprika
Pinch of oregano
Salt and pepper
85g/3 oz chorizo sausage, sliced thickly
150g/5 oz pasta shapes
"Free" side salad to serve

Soften onion and peppers in a saucepan sprayed with oil.

Stir in tomatoes, tomato purée, paprika, oregano and salt and pepper to taste. Bring to the boil, stirring. Turn down heat and simmer uncovered 10 minutes.

Cook pasta in lightly salted boiling water until just tender.

Stir chorizo into sauce and simmer another 5-10 minutes. Check seasoning.

Drain pasta and serve half to each person topped with half the sauce. Accompany with a "free" side salad.

Mediterranean

Chicken, Ham & Artichoke Pasta Bake

Serves 4

per serving   360   **14** 8

or 1 Booster Main Meal

225g/8 oz dried pasta bows or other pasta shapes
1 dspn olive oil
1 medium red pepper, de-seeded and diced
115g/4 oz chestnut mushrooms, sliced
295g can 99% fat-free condensed chicken soup
(e.g. Campbell's)
4 tbsp skimmed milk
400g can artichoke hearts, drained
60g/2 oz lean ham, chopped finely
Salt and black pepper
30g/1 oz fresh white breadcrumbs
60g/2 oz half-fat mature cheddar, grated
"Free" salad or vegetables to serve

Pre-heat oven to 200°C/gas mark 6.

Cook the pasta in lightly salted boiling water until just tender. Drain.

Heat the oil in a pan and stir-fry the pepper and mushrooms for 2 or 3 minutes until peppers are just beginning to soften.

Mix the chicken soup with the skimmed milk and stir into the pepper and mushroom mix, along with the artichoke hearts, ham and drained pasta. Season well and turn the mixture into an ovenproof dish.

Mix together the cheese and breadcrumbs, sprinkle on top and bake approximately 20 minutes or until top is golden.

Serve one-quarter of the bake to each person accompanied by "free" salad or vegetables.

Linguine Zarina

Serves 2

per serving   375   **15**   4

or 1 Main Meal

150g/5 oz linguine or spaghetti
100g/3½ oz smoked salmon pieces (e.g. Tesco Value)
2 heaped tbsp fat-free natural fromage frais
1 tbsp vodka
Salt and black pepper
2 tbsp chopped parsley
Lemon wedges to serve
"Free" side salad to serve

Have plates warmed, ready to serve.

Boil pasta in lightly salted boiling water until just tender.

Cut any large pieces of salmon into 1cm/½ inch strips.

When pasta is cooked, drain well. Return pasta to pan and immediately stir in smoked salmon, fromage frais, vodka, salt, plenty of black pepper and chopped parsley.

Serve each person with half the pasta with lemon wedges to squeeze over according to taste. Accompany with a "free" side salad.

Tagliatelle Verdi

Serves 2

per serving   400 **16** 5

or 1 Main Meal

175g/6 oz green tagliatelle
200g/7 oz trimmed weight leeks, sliced
2 tsp low-fat spread
200g pot fat-free fromage frais
Salt and pepper
2 dspn grated parmesan

Boil tagliatelle in lightly salted boiling water until just tender.

Place low-fat spread in a pan and melt gently. Add leeks and stir-fry until softened. Remove pan from heat and stir in fromage frais. Heat gently to warm through. Season with salt and pepper to taste.

Drain tagliatelle.

Serve each person with half the tagliatelle topped with half the sauce and 1 dspn grated parmesan sprinkled over.

Mediterranean

Pasta Puttanesca

Serves 2

per serving
370 **15** 6

or 1 Main Meal

50g can anchovy fillets in oil, well drained
2 cloves garlic, chopped
Spray oil
400g can tomatoes
1 tbsp tomato purée
Pinch of Italian seasoning or oregano
10 pitted black olives
175g/6 oz spaghetti, or other pasta
2 tsp capers
Salt and black pepper
"Free" green salad to serve

Chop the anchovies and gently fry together with the garlic in a saucepan sprayed with oil, about 1 minute.

Add the tomatoes, tomato purée, herbs and olives and stir well. Bring to the boil, then turn down the heat and simmer 15 minutes.

Meanwhile boil the pasta until just cooked.

Add capers and season the sauce.

Serve sauce poured over the drained pasta accompanied by a "free" green side salad.

Spaghetti Milanese

Serves 4

per serving

370 **15** 3

or 1 Main Meal

1 medium onion, chopped
1 stick celery, finely sliced
1 red or green pepper, chopped
1 clove garlic, peeled and crushed
150ml/¼ pint chicken or vegetable stock
400g can tomatoes, chopped
1 tbsp tomato purée
½ small glass wine
1 tsp oregano or marjoram
1 tsp sugar
350g/12 oz spaghetti, linguine or other pasta
115g/4 oz mushrooms, sliced
115g/4 oz lean ham, diced
Salt and black pepper
Chopped parsley to garnish

Place the onion, celery, peppers, garlic and stock into a saucepan. Bring to the boil, and cook approximately 7 minutes, or until vegetables are tender.

Stir in tomatoes, tomato purée, wine, herbs and sugar. Bring to the boil and then simmer approximately 30 minutes, stirring occasionally.

Meanwhile cook pasta in lightly salted boiling water until tender.

Add mushrooms to sauce and cook 3-4 minutes. Add ham and heat through gently. Season to taste.

Serve each person one-quarter of the drained pasta with one-quarter of the sauce, garnished with chopped parsley.

Mediterranean
Baked Penne

Serves 2

per serving   400   **16** 10

or 1 Main Meal

125g/4½ oz penne
1 small onion, finely chopped
1 small clove garlic, peeled and crushed
125g/4½ oz lean minced beef
400g can tomatoes
1 tbsp tomato purée
½ tsp oregano or mixed herbs
1 medium courgette, sliced
Salt and black pepper
1 egg, beaten
2 dspn grated parmesan
Spray oil
"Free" salad or vegetables to serve

Cook penne in lightly salted boiling water until just tender. Drain. Pre-heat oven to 200°C/gas mark 6.

Put onion, garlic and mince into a saucepan and stir-fry 5 mins. Cover and simmer 5 mins., stirring occasionally. Drain any excess fat. Stir in tomatoes, tomato purée, herbs and courgettes. Simmer, covered, 15 minutes. Stir and season. Remove from heat and stir in penne, beaten egg and parmesan.

Spray an ovenproof dish or roasting pan with oil. Fill with penne mixture and bake approximately 30 mins. or until penne is brown and crispy at the edges. Serve half the bake to each person accompanied by "free" salad or vegetables.

Serving suggestion

May also be eaten cold. Allow to cool and refrigerate, but serve at room temperature. One-quarter of the above recipe cut into slices and served with "free" salad makes a nice lunch.

per serving   200   **8** 5

or 1 Booster Quick Meal.

Mediterranean

Moules Marinière

Serves 1

per serving   200

| 600ml/about 1 pint mussels |
| 1 small onion, finely chopped |
| 1 tbsp chopped parsley |
| 1 glass white wine |
| ½ wine glass water |
| Salt and black pepper |

Scrub mussels and scrape off any beards. Discard any that are broken or open.

Put onion, parsley, wine, water and seasoning into a pan. Bring to the boil and simmer 5 minutes. Add mussels, cover pan and shake from time to time. After 5 minutes, mussels should be open. Discard any that remain closed.

Place mussels in a bowl with cooking liquor poured over.

Serving suggestion

Serve with 60g/2 oz crusty bread and a "free" side salad or vegetable dish.

per serving   350

or 1 Booster Main Meal

Italian Fish Topper

Serves 1

per serving   180   **7** **4**

150g/5 oz skinless cod steak
1 tbsp water or white wine
Salt and pepper.
30g/1 oz onion, finely chopped
5cm/2 in piece of celery, finely chopped
1 tomato, chopped
Pinch of Italian seasoning or mixed herbs
15g/½ oz half-fat cheese, grated
1 tbsp fresh wholemeal breadcrumbs

Pre-heat oven to 180°C/gas mark 4.

Place the cod and water or wine in an ovenproof dish, cover and bake approximately 20 minutes or until fish is opaque.

Meanwhile sweat the onion, celery, tomato and herbs in a small covered pan, stirring now and again. Add a little water if necessary.

Drain fish and place on a grill-proof plate. Top with vegetable mixture, grated cheese and breadcrumbs. Brown under a moderate grill.

Serving suggestion

Serve fish accompanied by 200g/7 oz boiled new potatoes topped with 1 tsp butter, and green beans or other "free" vegetables.

per serving   370   **15** **8**

or 1 Main Meal

Mediterranean
Seafood Paella

Serves 1

per serving

380   **15** 8

or 1 Main Meal

1 small onion, chopped
Handful of frozen sliced mixed peppers
Spray oil
½ chicken Oxo cube
275ml/ ½ pint hot water
1 tsp low-fat spread
1 small clove garlic, crushed
1/2 tsp turmeric
60g/2 oz rice
1 tomato, chopped
Handful of frozen sliced green beans
85g/3 oz white fish
60g/2 oz prawns or seafood mix, defrosted if frozen
5 pitted green or black olives (optional)
Salt and black pepper

Cook onions and peppers in a frying pan sprayed with oil until softened, stirring frequently. Dissolve Oxo in hot water.

Add low-fat spread to pan and allow to melt. Add garlic, turmeric and rice and stir well to coat with spread. Stir stock into pan. Cover and simmer gently 15 minutes.

Remove lid and add chopped tomato, green beans and white fish. If seafood is raw, also add now together with olives, if using. Cover and simmer 10-15 minutes. If seafood is pre-cooked (such as cooked frozen prawns or chopped seafood sticks), add these after 10 minutes and heat through just 1 minute, or they will become very rubbery. Season to taste.

Sole & Spinach Roulades

Serves 4

per serving   175   **7**

8 x 85g/3 oz sole fillets
1 level tsp fennel seeds, crushed lightly
Salt and pepper
8 spinach leaves, washed
1 tbsp dry white wine
Pinch of ground turmeric
3 tbsp 0% fat Greek yoghurt

Pre-heat oven to 180°C/gas mark 4 (or may be microwaved).

Sprinkle each sole fillet with fennel seeds, salt and pepper. Lay a spinach leaf on each, then roll up, tucking ends under.

Arrange in an ovenproof dish and sprinkle over wine. Cover and cook in oven 20 minutes, or microwave on high 6-7 minutes until tender.

Pour off cooking liquid into a small pan. Stir in turmeric and bring to the boil. Remove from heat and stir in Greek yoghurt. Serve sauce poured over fish.

Serving suggestion

Boil and mash 800g/1lb 12 oz potatoes, or boil 175g/6 oz rice. Serve each person with 2 roulades, one-quarter of the sauce and one-quarter of either the mashed potatoes or rice. Accompany with "free" vegetables.

per serving   325   **13**

or 1 Booster Main Meal

Mediterranean
Trout with Almonds

per serving   210   **8** 10

1 dspn flaked almonds
1 small whole trout approx.
q200-250g/7-9 oz, cleaned and fins removed
Lemon juice
Black pepper
Lemon wedges

Spread almonds in a pan and heat until lightly toasted, stirring frequently. (Flaked almonds can be bought ready toasted.)

Grill trout under moderate heat, turning once.

Remove skin from body area and transfer to serving plate. Sprinkle with lemon juice and black pepper and then with toasted almonds. Serve with additional lemon wedges.

Serving suggestion

Boil 200g/7 oz new potatoes and serve with trout together with green beans, broccoli or other "free" vegetables.

per serving   350   **14** 11

or 1 Booster Main Meal

Morroccan Fish Stew

Serves 2

per serving | 225 | **9** 5

350g/12 oz white fish and/or seafood mixture
1 tsp olive oil
1 small onion or shallot, chopped
1 clove garlic, peeled and crushed
½ tsp chilli powder
½ tsp cumin
400g can tomatoes
2 tbsp chopped coriander or parsley
Salt and pepper

Cut the fish into 4cm/1½ inch pieces.

Heat oil in a large saucepan and sauté onion until transparent. Add garlic and cook 1 minute. Add chilli and cumin and stir a few seconds more.

Stir in tomatoes and simmer 5 minutes. Add coriander or parsley, salt and pepper to taste and the pieces of fish or seafood. Cover and simmer gently 10 minutes or until fish is cooked. Check and stir now and again.

Serving suggestions

Put 100g/3½ oz couscous into a bowl or saucepan. Sprinkle over a pinch of salt and pour on 200ml/⅓ pint boiling water. Cover and leave 5 minutes for water to be absorbed. Fluff up with a fork and serve half to each person together with half the stew.

per serving | 400 | **16** 6

or 1 Main Meal

Piri Piri Chicken

Serves 2

per serving

380 **15** 5

or 1 Main Meal

2 skinless chicken breasts
1 clove garlic
1 red chilli, or to taste
1 red pepper
Spray oil
100g/3½ oz rice or pasta
1 small glass white wine
10 black olives
Salt and black pepper
Chopped parsley to garnish
"Free" vegetables or salad to serve

Cut the chicken breasts into thin strips. Finely chop the garlic. Remove seeds from the chilli and pepper and cut into strips.

Brown the chicken strips in pan sprayed with oil. Remove chicken.

In another saucepan, boil the rice or pasta.

Re-spray pan and cook the garlic, chilli and peppers until softened. Add the wine and bring to the boil. Add the chicken, olives and seasoning. Reduce heat, cover and simmer 10 minutes.

Drain the rice or pasta and serve half to each person with half the chicken. Garnish with chopped parsley and serve accompanied by "free" vegetables or salad.

Spinach & Feta Stuffed Chicken

Serves 4

per serving   260   **10** 8

2 tsp low-fat spread
3 shallots, chopped
100g/3½ oz baby spinach, chopped
100g/3½ oz feta, crumbled
Pinch dried oregano
Salt and pepper
4 skinless chicken breasts
2 tsp wholegrain mustard
100g/3½ oz 0% fat Greek yoghurt
Paprika to garnish, optional

Pre-heat oven to 190°C/gas mark 5.

Melt the low-fat spread in a pan and cook the shallots until soft. Stir in spinach and cook until wilted. Drain any excess liquid and place shallots and spinach in a bowl. Mix in crumbled feta and oregano and season to taste (take care as feta may be salty). Make deep incisions in the side of each chicken breast approx. 5cm/2 inches long. Spoon feta mixture into the incisions. Place in a roasting dish, cover with foil and bake 20-25 minutes.

Pour juices from dish into a saucepan. Re-cover chicken and keep warm. Boil juices 1-2 minutes to reduce. Remove from heat and stir in mustard and yoghurt. Cut each chicken breast into 5 slices and spoon sauce over to serve. Sprinkle with paprika to garnish (optional).

Serving suggestion

Boil 700g/1½ lb new potatoes. Serve each person with 1 sliced chicken breast, one-quarter of the sauce, one-quarter of the potatoes topped with 1 tsp low-fat spread. Accompany with broccoli or other "free" vegetables.

per serving   405   **16** 11

                                                      or 1 Main Meal

Mediterranean

Chicken Cordon Bleu

Serves 2

per serving   255   **10** 7

> 2 skinless, boneless chicken breasts
> 30g/1 oz mature half-fat cheddar
> 2 x 12-15g/½ oz thin slices lean
> smoked ham or proscuitto
> Spray oil
> 1 tsp cornflour
> 60ml/4 tbsp dry or medium sherry
> ½ Knorr chicken stock cube
> dissolved in 200ml/⅓ pint hot water
> Black pepper

Cut chicken breasts almost in half, horizontally. Open out and beat until about ½ cm/¼ inch thick. Cut cheese in half and wrap a slice of ham around each. Place one on each chicken breast, fold over and secure with wooden cocktail sticks.

Spray pan with oil and heat. Cook chicken breasts 10 minutes on one side, then turn over. Cover and cook a further 10-15 minutes on other side, until chicken is cooked through. Remove chicken and keep warm.

Mix cornflour to a smooth cream with 2 tbs cold water. Add sherry to pan and allow to bubble up. Add stock and cornflour cream to the pan and cook over medium heat, stirring continuously, until sauce has reduced and slightly thickened. Season with black pepper and serve poured over chicken breasts.

Serving suggestion

Boil and mash 350g/12 oz potatoes with a little skimmed milk. Stir in 2 dspn grated parmesan cheese and season to taste. Serve each person with 1 chicken breast, half the sauce, half the mashed potato and "free" vegetables.

per serving   410   **16** 10

                                              or 1 Main Meal

Greek Lemon Chicken

Serves 4

per serving   160   **6** 4

4 chicken leg quarters
1 large unwaxed lemon
Spray oil
1 medium onion, chopped
2 medium carrots, sliced
2 sticks celery, sliced
275ml/½ pint chicken or vegetable stock
2 tbsp chopped parsley
Salt and pepper

Remove skin from chicken and discard. Pare rind from lemon and cut into thin strips. Squeeze as much juice as you can from the lemon.

Spray a large saucepan with oil. Heat pan and cook chicken about 10 minutes. Remove chicken. Add onions, carrots and celery to pan. Cover and sweat gently about 10 minutes. Check now and again and add a little water if necessary to prevent sticking.

Return chicken to pan together with stock, lemon juice, lemon rind and parsley. Season to taste. Bring to a simmer, cover and cook very gently 30 minutes.

Serving suggestion

Boil 700g/1½ lb new potatoes. Serve each person with one-quarter of the recipe, one-quarter of the potatoes and additional "free" vegetables.

per serving   290   **12** 5

or 1 Quick Meal
or 1 Booster Main Meal

Tuscan Turkey Paesana

Serves 4

per serving   275   **11**

---

4 x 85g/3 oz turkey escalopes
1 medium egg, beaten
85g/3 oz fresh white breadcrumbs
2 tsp olive oil
1 medium onion, finely chopped
1 clove garlic, crushed
700g/1½ lb tomatoes, peeled and chopped
1 tbsp tomato purée
1 tbsp freshly chopped basil
Salt and black pepper
1 tbsp olive oil
125g pack mozzarella light, sliced
Sprigs of fresh basil to garnish

Dip the escalopes in beaten egg then coat in breadcrumbs.

Now make the sauce. Heat the 2 tsp olive oil and gently fry the onion and garlic until soft but not browned. Add the tomatoes, tomato purée, basil and seasoning and cook gently 15 minutes. Check seasoning.

Heat 1 tbsp olive oil in a large shallow pan and cook the breaded escalopes for about 3 minutes each side, or until tender. Transfer to grill rack.

Top with mozzarella, grill until cheese melts and serve on a bed of sauce, garnished with basil.

Serving suggestion

Boil 150g/5 oz rice. Serve each person with 1 escalope, one-quarter of the sauce, one-quarter of the rice and "free" vegetables.

per serving   410   **16** 12

or 1 Main Meal

Cheat's Chicken Provencale

Serves 2

per serving   255   **10** 9

or 1 Booster Quick Meal

| 4 skinless chicken thighs |
| 400g approx. can ratatouille |

Pre-heat oven to 190°C/gas mark 5.

Place chicken thighs and ratatouille in an ovenproof dish. Cover and bake approximately 20-25 minutes or until chicken is cooked through.

Serving suggestion

Boil 85g/3 oz rice or pasta shapes. Serve each person with 2 chicken thighs, half the ratatouille and half the rice or pasta.

per serving   405   **16** 10

or 1 Main Meal

Mediterranean
Turkey Koftas

Serves 4

per serving of 2 koftas   150   **6** 6

8 wooden kebab skewers
450g/1 lb turkey mince
1 medium onion, grated
2 cloves garlic, peeled and crushed
1 tsp ground coriander
1 tsp ground cumin
2 tbsp chopped parsley or coriander
Salt and black pepper
Spray oil

Soak the kebab skewers in water 30 minutes.

Place all the ingredients (except spray oil) into a food processor and blitz 1-2 minutes, or until the mixture comes together. Alternatively, knead together in a mixing bowl until it forms a ball in the centre of the bowl.

Divide the mixture into 8 then carefully mould round the kebab sticks, pressing the mixture firmly into a sausage shape.

Pre-heat the grill.

Spray a baking sheet with oil and place the koftas on it. Spray the koftas with oil. Place the baking sheet under the grill and grill 8-10 minutes, or until thoroughly cooked. Turn occasionally during grilling and spray with a little oil if necessary.

Serving suggestion

Serve each person with 2 koftas, 1 warmed pitta bread and "free" salad.

per serving   300   **12** 8

or 1 Quick Meal

Lamb with Apricots & Couscous

Serves 1

per serving   325 **13** 9

or 1 Booster Main Meal

1 small onion, chopped
Spray oil
85g/3 oz lean lamb
Pinch of cinnamon
Pinch of cumin
1 tsp turmeric
150ml/¼ pint stock
4 ready-to-eat apricots
45g/1½ oz couscous
"Free" vegetables to serve

Spray pan with oil and heat. Add onion and stir-fry until soft, adding a little water now and again to prevent sticking.

Cut lamb into small cubes and add to pan. Stir-fry a few minutes until lamb is browned and cooked through.

Add spices and stir 30 seconds to warm through. Stir in stock and apricots. Bring to the boil, cover and simmer 2-3 minutes. Turn off heat and stir couscous into pan. Replace cover and leave 2-3 minutes for couscous to swell and absorb juices. Fluff up with a fork before serving with "free" vegetables.

Mediterranean
Beef Bourguignon

Serves 2

per serving   200 **8** 7

175g/6 oz trimmed weight, lean steak
60g/2 oz lean ham
115g/4 oz button mushrooms
1 small onion, finely sliced
2 bay leaves
½ tsp Herbes de Provence or mixed herbs
1 tbsp tomato purée
2 tbsp red wine
1 beef Oxo cube
275ml/½ pint hot water
1 tsp cornflour (optional)

Pre-heat oven to 180°C/gas mark 4.

Cut steak into cubes and ham into small strips. Cut mushrooms into halves or quarters if large.

Place steak, ham, mushrooms, onions, bay leaves and herbs into an ovenproof casserole.

Crumble Oxo cube into a jug and add tomato purée and wine. Pour in hot water and stir to dissolve Oxo. Pour this mixture into the casserole. Cover tightly and cook in the oven 2 hours, or until meat is tender.

If you prefer a thicker gravy, put cornflour into a small pan and mix with 1 tbsp water. Add juices from the casserole. Bring to the boil, stirring continuously, until thickened.

Serving suggestion

Boil 85g/3 oz rice. Serve half the casserole to each person with half the rice, accompanied by "free" vegetables.

per serving   350 **14** 8

or 1 Booster Main Meal

Saltimbocca

per serving   150   6 3

> 2 x 60g/2 oz thin pork escalopes
> 2 wafer thin slices smoked ham or proscuitto
> 2 sage leaves or 4 basil leaves
> Spray oil

If necessary, beat out escalopes until about ½ cm/¼ inch thick.

Place a slice of ham and 1 sage leaf or 2 basil leaves on each. Fold over and secure with wooden cocktail sticks.

Spray a pan with oil and heat. Fry the escalopes approximately 5-7 minutes each side, or until cooked through.

Serving suggestion

Boil and drain 45g/1½ oz tagliatelle or pasta shapes. Serve the saltimbocca with the pasta and 150ml/¼ pint warmed low-fat "healthy" pasta sauce and "free" vegetables, or "free" side salad sprinkled with balsamic vinegar.

per serving   375   **15** 6

or 1 Main Meal

Scottish Slimmers/Weight Management/Slimming Magazine Clubs | 39

Pork Escalopes Marsala

Serves 1

per serving 175 **7**

2 x 60g/2 oz pork escalopes
Spray oil, preferably olive oil flavour
½ tsp stock powder
(e.g. Marigold Vegetable or Knorr Chicken)
60ml/2 fl.oz boiling water
2 tbsp marsala or medium/sweet sherry
Chopped parsley to garnish (optional)

If necessary, beat out escalopes until about ½ cm/¼ inch thick.

Spray pan with oil and heat. Fry escalopes a few minutes on each side, until just cooked through. Remove from pan and keep warm.

Dissolve stock powder in boiling water and add to pan together with the marsala or sherry. Boil approximately 2 minutes, stirring and scraping meat residue, until reduced by one-third.

Pour pan juices over escalopes and garnish with chopped parsley (optional).

Serving suggestion

Drain a 300g can of new potatoes. Place on grill rack and spray lightly with oil. Brown under a hot grill approximately 20 minutes, turning and re-spraying halfway through. Serve the potatoes with the escalopes and "free" vegetables.

Per serving 300 **12**

or 1 Quick Meal
or 1 Booster Main Meal

Beef Olives

Serves 4

per serving   210

1 medium onion, sliced
2 medium carrots, sliced
2 sticks celery, sliced
400g can tomatoes
1 Knorr beef stock cube
4 tbsp red or white wine
2 bay leaves
4 thin slices lean braising steak, approximately 85g/3 oz each
4 Wall's Lean Recipe Sausages, skins removed
2 tbsp sage and onion stuffing mix
½ tsp dried Herbes de Provence or mixed herbs
Salt and pepper

Pre-heat oven to 170°C/gas mark 3.

Sweat onions, carrots and celery in a little water approx. 10 mins. Transfer to an ovenproof casserole. Stir in tomatoes, crumbled stock cube, wine and bay leaves.

Pre-heat grill. If necessary, beat out slices of steak to flatten. Place skinned sausages in a bowl and mix in stuffing and herbs. Spread quarter of the mix on each piece of steak, roll up and secure with a cocktail stick. Brown under grill.

Add rolls to casserole. Cover tightly and cook 2½ - 3 hours or until very tender. If dry, stir in a little hot water. Check seasoning and remove cocktail sticks before serving.

Serving suggestion

Boil and mash 800g/1¾ lb potatoes with a little skimmed milk. Serve each person with 1 beef roll, one-quarter of the sauce, one-quarter of the mash and "free" green vegetables.

per serving   370

or 1 Main Meal

Moussaka

Serves 2

per serving

300   **12** (14)

1 Quick Meal

200g/7 oz lean beef mince
1 onion, chopped
1 clove garlic, peeled and crushed
400g can tomatoes, chopped
1 tbsp tomato purée
¼ tsp marjoram
Pinch oregano
Freshly grated nutmeg
Salt and pepper
1 medium aubergine, sliced
2 level dspn cornflour
275ml/½ pint skimmed milk
60g/2 oz feta
"Free" salad or green vegetables to serve

Stir-fry mince, onion and garlic until browned. Cover and simmer gently 10 minutes. Drain off any surplus fat. Stir in tomatoes, tomato purée, marjoram, oregano and freshly grated nutmeg. Bring to the boil, then lower heat and simmer 10-15 minutes. Season to taste.

Meanwhile, boil the aubergine slices approximately 3 minutes to soften. Drain, and place on kitchen paper to absorb excess moisture.

Pre-heat oven to 190°C/gas mark 5.

Put cornflour and milk in a saucepan and bring to the boil, stirring continuously until sauce thickens. Season with salt and pepper.

Layer aubergine slices and mince and tomato mix in an ovenproof casserole. Top with white sauce and crumbled feta. Bake approximately 40 minutes.

Serve each person with half the moussaka accompanied by "free" salad or vegetables.

Crêpes Suzette-style

serves 2, per serving	255	**10** 10
serves 3, per serving	170	7 7

60g/2 oz plain flour
Tiny pinch of salt
1 medium egg
150ml/¼ pint skimmed milk
Spray oil
1 tbsp low-fat spread
150ml/¼ pint unsweetened orange juice
Grated zest of 1 small orange
1 tbsp Cointreau, Grand Marnier, brandy or sherry
2 dspn granulated sweetener, or to taste

Sift flour and salt into a mixing bowl. Make a well in the centre and break egg into the well. Beat the egg, gradually incorporating some of the flour. Add some of the milk, beating in more of the flour. Continue to add milk and incorporate more flour until everything is well mixed together. The batter should be like thin cream.

Spray a 15-18 cm/6-7" pan with oil and heat until just starting to smoke. Add about 2 tbsp batter to the pan and swirl round to cover base of pan. Cook until golden underneath. Flip over, or toss, and cook other side.

Slide onto a warm plate and cover with foil until remaining pancakes are cooked. Re-spray pan between each pancake. Makes 6 pancakes.

Put low-fat spread into pan and melt gently. Stir in orange juice, grated zest and 1 tbsp Cointreau, Grand Marnier, brandy or sherry. Bring to the boil, stirring. Stir in granulated sweetener to taste. Fold pancakes in quarters, add to pan. Turn down heat, spoon sauce over and in-between pancakes and warm through.

Cappuccino Cream

Serves 4

per serving   150   6

> 2 tsp instant coffee
> 1 tbsp boiling water
> 500g tub quark skimmed milk soft cheese
> 4 dspn granulated sweetener, or to taste
> 1 tbsp Amaretto Disaronno
> or other liqueur, or brandy
> 4 swirls half-fat aerosol cream
> (e.g. Anchor Light Real Dairy Cream)
> 1 square dark chocolate

Place chocolate in fridge, so that it is easier to grate.

Dissolve the coffee in the boiling water. Stir into the quark, together with the granulated sweetener and liqueur. Mix well.

Divide the mixture between 4 wineglasses or ramekins.

Just before serving, place a swirl of half-fat aerosol cream on each dessert and grate over a little dark chocolate.

Serving suggestion

2 Doria Amaretti biscuits, per serving   50   2

Pear & Ratafia Flan

Serves 4

per serving   175   **7**   2

75g small, fluted sponge flan case
100g/3½ oz fat-free fromage frais
3-4 drops vanilla essence
1 tbsp granulated sweetener, or to taste
1 dspn sherry
410g can pears in juice, drained
1 sachet low-calorie chocolate drink powder (e.g. Cadbury's High Lights)
1 tbsp boiling water
30g/1 oz ratafia biscuits, crushed

Cut flan case across horizontally (to make 2 sponges). Mix fromage frais with vanilla essence and sweetener to taste. Spread mixture over base half of flan and place the other half on top (with the "indented" side uppermost).

Sprinkle sherry over the "indent" and arrange pears on top. Mix chocolate powder with boiling water to make a sauce and spoon over the pears. Scatter crushed ratafia over the pears and chocolate.

Best made a few hours in advance and chilled in the fridge.

Mediterranean
Black Cherry Zabaglione

Serves 4

per serving   150   6

425g can pitted black cherries in syrup (e.g John West)
4 medium egg yolks
2 dspn sugar
2 tbsp Marsala or sweet sherry
1 tbsp chopped nuts, lightly toasted

Heat cherries through gently in a saucepan or microwave. Drain thoroughly, cover and keep warm.

Bring a pan with about 1 cm/½ inch water to a gentle simmer.

Using a bowl which will rest comfortably on the pan without touching the bottom, and preferably an electric whisk, start whisking the eggs, sugar and Marsala or sherry until frothy (off the heat).

Rest the bowl over the pan of simmering water and continue whisking about 7 minutes until thick, pale and leaving a trail. Keep water at a gentle simmer throughout.

Divide the warm cherries between 4 wine glasses or small ramekins. Spoon zabaglione over the top, sprinkle with toasted nuts and serve immediately.

Serving suggestion

Substitute the cherries for 250g/9 oz chopped fresh fruit or 400-425g can of fruit in juice, such as grapes, peaches or apricots. Sprinkle each portion with 1 tsp of your favourite liqueur before spooning over zabaglione. This will add about 15 calories or ½ Check per serving.

Or, replace chopped nuts with 3 baby ratafia or 1 Doria Amaretti biscuit per serving. Calories and Checks remain approximately the same, but fat grams reduce to 6.

Mediterranean

Stuffed peaches

Serves 4

per serving   160   **6** 5

4 large ripe peaches
85g/3 oz marzipan
1 tbsp flaked almonds, lightly toasted

Pre-heat oven to 180°C/gas mark 4.

Blanch the peaches in boiling water about 45 seconds. Take out and remove skins. If peaches are not quite ripe and still difficult to peel, use a vegetable peeler to peel thinly.

Cut in half and remove stones. Place 4 halves, cut side up in an ovenproof dish.

Cut the marzipan into 4 pieces, roll into small balls and place on the peach halves. Top with remaining peach halves, gently pressing together. Pierce a wooden cocktail stick through each peach to hold the two halves together. Cover and bake approx.20-25 mins.

Remove cocktail sticks. Serve warm, scattered with almond flakes. Or, allow to cool and chill in the refrigerator. Scatter with almonds just before serving.